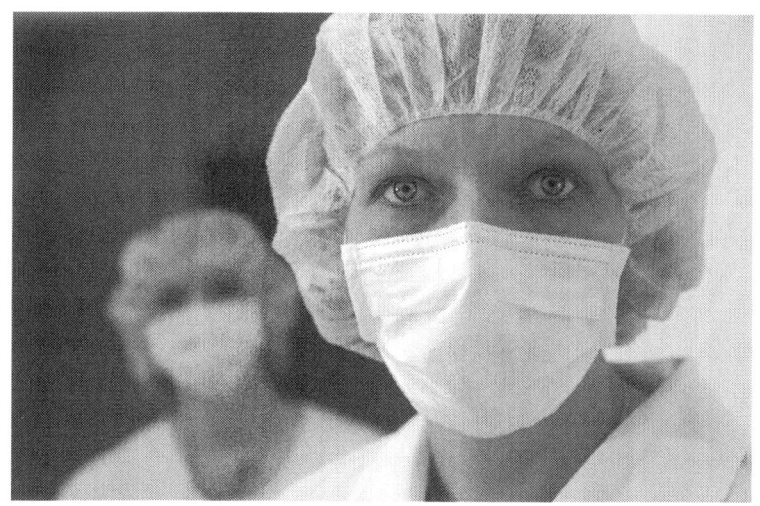

A DAY IN THE LIFE

MEDICAL DEVICE AND PHARMACEUTICAL SALES

BY BILL MITCHELL

EXPERIENCE THE INDUSTRY

A Day In the Life

Medical Device and Pharmaceutical Sales

THIRD EDITION

© COPYRIGHT 2012 ALL RIGHTS RESERVED

Table of Contents

Introduction 6

The Basis 8

The Beginning 11

The First Week 13

Training and Orientation 16

Territory 21

Travel 26

Quotas 29

Perks 33

Compensation 37

Spiffs 41

Awards 45

Competition 48

The Office 52

Typical Day 56

Covering a Hospital 62

Tracking Sales and Notes (CRM) 67

Product Specialists 70

Meetings 73

Trade Shows 77

Sales Funnel 79

Quotes 83

Sales 87

Image and Professionalism 91

Vacation 93

Expenses 96

SUMMARY 99

INTRODUCTION

Medical Device Sales and Pharmaceutical Sales are businesses that are highly sought after as they typically generate some of the highest salaries in business.

It is a hot industry that everyone talks about but many people are left wondering what it is like to actually work in the business. What do these representatives do on a daily basis? What is our job like? How is the job performed? What expectations are there and what perks do you receive?

In this book we are going to take an insider's look into exactly what it is like to work in Medical Device Sales and Pharmaceutical Sales for those of you that are considering entering this business or are just curious about the industry. We will look at this business from the eyes of a representative that has worked in both Pharmaceutical Sales and Medical Device Sales and for some of the largest companies in the world as well as a couple smaller ones.

It is a Day in the Life in this profession and you are along for the ride!

THE BASIS

When you were little, did you ever see people go to work and wonder what they did for a living? You saw them dressed up, get in their cars and go to some unknown business for some unknown reason. Even when you may have asked a person what they did for a living, many times you still probably walked away without a good sense of what they actually did on a daily basis.

Fast forward until now, you may be considering Medical Device or Pharmaceutical Sales but you still might not have a firm sense for what this business is like. You may be wondering about the real income potential, the different perks of the job, what an average day will be like, and what this profession really entails? In other words, what is a day in the life in this business?

This is what we are going to explore together in this book. We are going to let you peer into the industry with clarity via the perspective of someone who has worked in the industry for multiple companies of varying sizes and types. If you are serious about entering this business, this journey and preparation is probably going to be some of the best time you can possibly spend preparing yourself.

Ultimately, this book will allow you to eliminate the surprises that would frequently accompany a new hire in this industry because you already know what to expect. If you read this book before the interview process, you will be miles ahead of others starting out and notably ahead of those you are competing against.

Also, we are going to give you a couple of perspectives. I want you to see what a day in the life is like when you first start, and then when you are more established since these phases are very different. We are also going to give you a more thorough look at many of the different things you will encounter during your time with a company over the course of a year.

This profession is one of the absolutely greatest jobs in business and so let's dive in together and I will give you the grand tour.

THE BEGINNING

When you first get your offer to join a new Medical Device or Pharmaceutical company, you will be on top of the world. You made it through the gauntlet of applications, interviews, and finally received your offer.

You will unquestionably be filled with feelings of excitement, joy, and enthusiasm. However, these feelings will most likely be flanked by feelings of anxiousness since you don't know what to expect. Not to worry, these feeling are natural. However, after reading this book, you will have a much better handle on what lies ahead of you and what your job will really entail so you will feel less anxious about the process.

THE FIRST WEEK

Just like any job, once you are hired, it all starts with some good old fashion paperwork. Insurance forms, non-disclosures, 401k, etc. will undoubtedly consume your first few days. You will also have several stacks of company policies to read and agree to.

During this time, you will primarily work with the Human Resource department and a person who is responsible for the on-boarding of new representatives.

You will also receive your laptop, possibly an iPad and your email box will be activated. Almost immediately, you will begin to hear from people at the company including training resources and of course your managers (who you probably met during the interview process). During this stage, everyone is going to be congratulating you, welcoming you on-board, and providing some direction.

Along with your laptop, you will also receive your new cell phone which you will most likely need to activate and get synched with the internal network. There are clear instructions provided by the company for doing this but contact information for the I.T. department will also be included in case you get stuck.

Your business cards will be printed, and you will be given many new internal directories.

The first week will seem like a blur but it is all a part of getting you ready to roll and take on your brand new and exciting career in this business.

TRAINING AND ORIENTATION

It is not unexpected that the next phase of the process is training and orientation. While the standard company forms are pretty much the same no matter the company, training and orientation is where you start to see vast differences among companies.

Generally speaking, large companies tend to have a more formal and regimented training process prior to sending you into the field while smaller companies tend to do more on the job training.

The amount of training you receive will also somewhat depend on what products you are carrying. For instance, it is not uncommon for pharmaceutical companies to send their new hires through several weeks of classroom training with somewhat rigorous and on-going testing and certification.

Large medical device companies tend to have a week or so of classroom training with a multitude of on-line training and certifications. The on-line certifications are frequent and required throughout the year for all employee's in both industries so it is something to get used to.

In both cases, you will typically be joined by new hires from across the country and in some cases, across the world. You may also find that your training is delayed just slightly from your start date as most companies try to align new training classes to optimize efficiency.

Smaller companies do not have the number of simultaneous on-boarding candidates or resources to provide such a robust training program. Consequently, it is more likely that you will experience a greater amount of on the job training or shadowing of fellow representatives.

In fact, I remember my first medical device sales job. I was hired by a smaller company to sell cardiac monitoring products to a host of hospitals and cardiologist. At the time, it was my first endeavor into this industry and since a book like this didn't exist, I had absolutely no idea what to expect. In my case, there was no formalized training program at all since it was a small company in transition. So what did I do, I simply picked up the product manuals and started reading. Fortunately at the time, I didn't know any better so I didn't know what I was missing. It was a funny way of learning but I found some good tips along the way that I can share with you in case you find yourself in this situation.

There are many of you that pick up this book that will begin working for a smaller company that doesn't have an official training program. It can be intimidating at first but let me share a few valuable secrets with you that will make your life much easier. After reading the manual, find a customer that is using your product and ask them if you can shadow them for a day. You will find that almost all of your customers are more than happy to have you alongside of them and you can learn more in a day from them then you could learn in a week of almost any other kind of training.

Another important secret is to shadow another sales representative. The representatives around you are generally willing to help a new hire and can help you learn about the approach, strengths and weaknesses of your products, competition, internal structure, etc.

Also, as you start to transition into your role, remember that it is perfectly acceptable to tell your customers that you don't know the answer to a specific question. Simply admit that you are new and tell them that you will find the answer to their question and will loop back with them.

TERRITORY

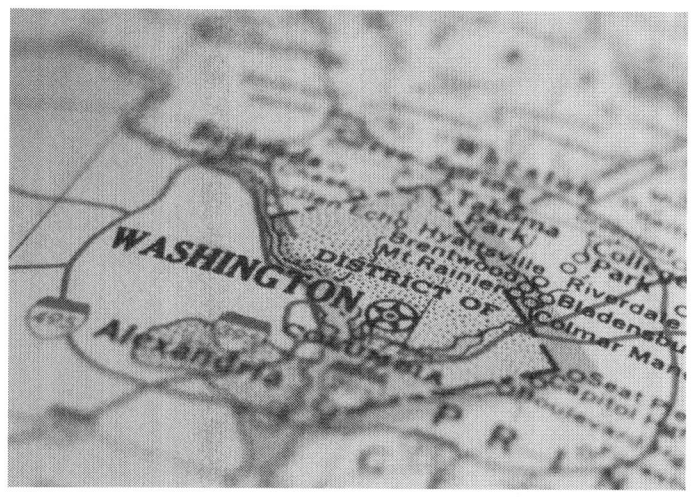

Territories among companies are extremely diverse depending on the type of company, product, size of company, etc. For instance, a person at a large company that is selling high end and high dollar equipment may have only thirty hospitals and a multitude of offices and imaging centers within a small geographic area (such as a section of the state or a large city).

On the other hand, if you are working for a small company selling patient monitors for instance, you may be covering three or four states and have several hundred customers.

Pharmaceutical sales works the same way; Some representatives have several states with hundreds of customers while others have only a handful of very high volume and lucrative customers.

No matter what size of territory you have, your list of customers will become your highest priority as these are the people that will help you succeed in your career and will be the source of your income.

One of the first things that you will do in your job is send out an introductory announcement to your customers explaining that you are their new representative. You will want to list your product(s), provide your contact information, and let them know that you are there for them should they have any needs. It can be short and sweet but it is an important step.

You also need to know what is going on in your territory. What action items are currently open? What sales are pending? Who needs what? And how can you optimize your time? It is a crazy period but you want to devote yourself to understanding what is needed so that you can be sure that none of your customers are neglected.

You will be all of a sudden embedded with a million things to do since you need to get your arms around the territory. However, keep in mind that this is a temporary period of craziness that gets easier every day you work in the territory.

You should also know that not all territories are created equal. Companies hire new representatives for a variety of reasons. Some are due to promotions within the company or people leaving for a perceived better opportunity. However, quite frequently, a company will hire a new representative in a territory due to a historical lack of performance or lack of business in this territory.

In other words, it is possible that the previous representative either wasn't doing their job or had trouble building the territory for any variety of reasons.

What this means is that you will not automatically be walking into a situation where your territory is churning large amounts of business. This is perfectly OK and is actually expected since it is so common. The good thing about this business is that with some work, you can shape a territory and just because it wasn't good before, doesn't mean that it can't be on top next year.

When I started my first job, the territory I had was the worst territory in the company for the previous seven years. When I left, it was consistently in the top three. It wasn't luck, it was hard work and dedication.

If you are fortunate enough to land a territory that is always producing, you need to quickly get on top of it so you don't miss a beat in your customers eyes. This sounds really obvious, however, so many people get so overwhelmed with the on-boarding process that they put off their customers until well after they are settled into the new job.

TRAVEL

Traveling is a topic that is very polarized but it is generally a part of this business to some degree. Some feel that the more travel the better, while others want to minimize their travel. No matter what your opinion, there will be some sort of travel at some point.

It stands to reason that the size of your territory and amount of expected customer face time indicates the amount of travel that is required. Clearly, if you are covering four states, you will likely be on the road more frequently than if you are covering only one large city. However, when we discuss travel, you must differentiate between overnight and daily travel.

Typically, the amount of travel is specified in the job description. However, this travel percentage is usually written in terms of overnight travel. So 80% travel would mean that you would be on the road four of the five days. However, there is also daily travel that is not usually listed as a percentage. In sales, you generally want to maximize your face time with your customers. Thus, you will probably be in accounts on a daily basis but will return home at the end of the day.

As you will learn in later chapters, a day in the life of an established representative is typically going between appointments or calls. Thus, you are typically on the move (which is great news if you don't like being trapped behind a desk).

Whether you are traveling far or staying regionally, we always try to optimize the route. A good way to do this is through Microsoft MapPoint to visualize where your stops are and then find ways to maximize the time in the targeted area. For instance, if I am traveling ninety miles away, who else can I see in that area or who can I visit on the way to or way back from this area to make the most of my time on the road?

Planning your travel strategically will make sure that you optimize your time so that you can make the most money.

QUOTAS

Nobody likes a quota but quotas are something that you must live with in sales. Every company, both large and small, maintains sales targets and goals. It is of course the responsibility of the sales force to help achieve these goals.

As everyone know, sales revenues are necessary to continue running the business. So for instance, there is a minimum dollar figure that the company needs to keep the lights on, pay salaries, manufacture products, etc. In addition, there is profit needed to continue research and develop products, expand operations, etc. Then there are growth targets or the amount the company would like to grow in any given year. All of these numbers are assimilated, divided into quotas, and then distributed among the sales team.

The Regional Managers are typically responsible for dividing up quotas among the territories based on the business opportunity in a specific territory. For instance, if I have 100 hospitals and my neighboring territory has 200 hospitals, it stands to reason that their quota will be higher than mine. However, previous performance, installed base, etc. all play into this so their quota may not necessarily be twice as much. While many calculations are made, the division of quotas can be considered an art rather than an exact science.

In any case, our job naturally is to sell as much as we can in a given year to achieve our quota (a quota that typically gets higher by the year). When you first get your quota, be prepared for a little sticker shock.

I remember when I received my first quota. I recall thinking to myself, how can I sell over a million dollars worth of equipment??? However, it is achievable and as the years unfold and you begin making sales and money, you will be amazed at what you can do.

Most companies have tiered quota compensation packages that allow you to be paid expedientially if you blow out your quota. For instance, you might make 20% more per sale after you achieve 100% of your quota. This is truly when you can earn incredible money and it helps keep you very motivated when you are approaching your target.

Quota categories are also something that you may have to contend with if you sell several products. Some companies expect you to meet sales objectives in all product categories (AKA, achieve quota for every product you sell) in order to maximize your revenue. Thus, you may sell enough dollars to meet your overall quota number, however, if you didn't achieve what is called "Balanced Selling" or selling in all product categories, then you might not make as much as you could have.

As you can see, these structures can be very complex but the general idea is to keep you motivated and give the company a measure to gauge you. If you are anything like me, you try to sell as much as possible every year to make as much money as possible irrespective of what number is given to you.

PERKS

There are so many nice perks of this business that make it even more attractive. If you have had some of these perks before, they may not seem so special but if you have not, you will absolutely love them!

For instance, your cell phone, phone/data/texting plan is paid for by the company. The company knows you need a phone to conduct business and provides you one at no cost. This means one more personal bill that you can discontinue at home.

You are issued a laptop which is also nice even if you have a computer. Along with that laptop, your company will typically reimburse for home internet charges (if you do not report to an office) and may also offer an internet air card so you can connect to the internet from anywhere.

While these are nice little perks, there are bigger ones!

For instance, many companies provide you with a company car. After all, you are expected to drive for the company so it makes sense that they give you a vehicle to get the job done. The type of car is typically what I call mid-size so it is usually a Chevy Impala, Ford Fusion, Chrysler 300, etc. and they are typically moderately equipped. Depending on your company, you may even get to choose the car type in the class (for instance Impala or Fusion) and even the color combination.

All maintenance, insurance, and fuel are covered by the company. Rules vary for personal use but usually the company does not mind if you use the company car for reasonable personal use which can save you a lot of money and better your household bottom line even more.

These cars are used in the fleet for approximately 75,000 miles and then you will be issued a new one. Some companies even let you purchase the car for a bargain price at the end of term if you want it for personal use (some choose to give it to their children or spouse).

Some of the smaller companies can't afford to acquire and maintain a fleet of vehicles so they will give you a monthly car allowance with a fuel card or will pay you the government mileage rate. Thus, unless you work for an extremely small and financially struggling Medical Device or Pharmaceutical company, you should expect a vehicle or vehicle allowance which is a great perk.

Medical Device Sales and Pharmaceutical Sales usually come with some very nice perks, but one of the greatest perks is freedom of scheduling. While you are being evaluated by your managers, you don't have a manager watching your every move and you get to choose where you go and how to use your time (to a certain extent). This means that you can flex your schedule to make personal commitments if necessary.

Some weeks will be busier than others (as we will discuss later), but generally speaking, you have the latitude to make your job align with certain commitments (which is sometimes important for working parents who need to attend an occasional appointment or such). I always think of my job like I am running my own little business and I get to call the shots.

COMPENSATION

So let's talk about the fun part, COMPENSATION! The great thing about Medical Device Sales is that the money can be substantial. In fact, at some of the larger companies with the higher end product lines, there are always several people clearing $500,000 per year.

While some very entry level jobs may offer a commission only model, most medical device sales jobs offer a base salary plus a commission plan.

The base salary is especially valuable in the beginning of your time with a company but it is the commission that helps you earn the big money.

The base can vary widely but the range is generally $50,000 - $70,000. This is probably a good median number for most of the moderate medical device positions. Pharmaceutical companies tend to offer larger bases but don't have the higher commission structures.

Many companies also have compensation structures where your base salary will increase as you are with the company longer. For instance, at one company I worked with, my base was 50,000 when I was hired but moved up to $80,000 by the time I was moving to my next job.

Some of you may be looking at the base salary with great excitement but the most exciting part is that the base salary should be the smaller portion of your income.

Commissions vary widely so it is entirely up to the company that you are working for. If you sell very high end equipment, it may be 1%. For others it may be 5% or 10%. In pharmaceuticals, it is generally tied to territory growth. It really depends but you should expect an after tax paycheck in the thousands every month (typically on the last Friday of the month).

For Medical Device companies, typically commissions are paid out partially when the unit is sold and then the remainder when the unit ships. What is nice about this model is that once you get your territory moving, you will have a constant stream of income.

Another great thing is that commissions are generally not capped. In one instance in my career, I sold the largest sale in the history of the company and was seeing regular five figure pay checks. In fact, I remember checking my direct deposit once to see an after tax deposit of $30,000 (in a single check). There is definitely money to be made which is why so many people pursue this business.

Many people ask me, what should I expect for a median salary when I first get started with a company. While this is a difficult question to answer, for many decent medical device jobs you will be seeing a total take home package of about $110,000 - $130,000 while many of the pharmaceutical salaries will be closer to the $100,000 mark. However, these numbers are variable and a lot of it depends on your success, territory dynamics, sales cycle, company, product, etc.

SPIFFS

The base salary and commissions are not the only way we get paid. There are frequently spiff programs going on. A spiff is simply another word for incentive that is offered for selling a product or generating a product lead that translates into a sale.

For instance, you may get a $1,000 spiff for any widget sales closed in Q2. Or sometimes there are lead generation spiff's where you get $500 for any widget lead that translates into a sale.

Depending on the company goals, spiff's are used to drive business in a particular area. So for instance, if the company wants to boost service sales, there may be a $750 spiff for every service contract sold.

Also, there can be many different spiffs in place at the same time. It is also possible for other companies to pay you these spiffs depending on the corporate relationships that are in place.

The spiff's can be large too. I have seen them as high as $6,000. Depending on the number of spiffs and your success in the area, you may find that they really add up. In fact, Spiffs may account for 10% of your total income.

Sales contests are also frequently run to keep motivation up. The contest can have any parameter that a company wishes. It can be the top representative of the quarter, top in a product category, or any way they choose to position it. The prize can also be anything from a TV, gift card, stock, cash, to just about anything else.

The most unusual contest that encountered was from a smaller company that offered a lease on a Porsche Boxster for anyone that sold a certain threshold of a certain high margin product. The threshold was so high that it was difficult to imagine that anyone would do it but it was indeed done and a rep had a new Boxster lease for three years.

These types of incentives are sort of games and they really make it fun and help you get excited and motivated to get that prize. Beware though; your spouse or significant other may all of a sudden become a second manager when they hear about the nice prizes that they would like to have. In any case, we love our spiff's.

AWARDS

Another great perk of Medical Device and Pharmaceutical Sales is the way the best representatives are treated. In a typical company, an award trip is place to incentivize the sales force. Usually the top three or five grossing sales representatives are invited on these trips as are their spouses.

These trips can range from Florida to Europe or beyond. They can be luxurious cruises or anything else depending on the company. You and your spouse (or guest) are treated like gold on these trips and all expenses are taken care of. I can tell you from personal experience that these trips are so much fun.

I remember two trips in particular, one to Barcelona where we stayed on the beautiful coast and ate at magnificent restaurants. And another that I fondly remember was Los Cabos, Mexico where our suite was overlooking the crystal clear waters and every thoughtful detail was considered.

There are even award ceremonies for selling the most in a product category (if you have more than one) which usually translates into a prize like a gift certificate.

The very top sales representative of the company will usually also win a major prize which can be anything from a gift certificate, to a consumer electronic to a Rolex. If the company is public, a token stock gift is also usually gifted.

As you can see, there is a lot of money to be made and a lot of ways to make it. This is part of the reason why this business is so attractive to so many and so addictive to those already in it.

COMPETITION

In this industry, there is a tremendous amount of competition that surrounds you. First, you face your traditional competition; other companies that sell competing products. In this business, there is never a day when your competition isn't trying to outthink, outmaneuver, and overtake you. This means that you must constantly be on the offense and defense to win the business that you are pursuing and protect the business that you already have.

Being better than your competition is a must. If your products aren't better, then learning how to sell more effectively and building stronger customer relationships are key elements in helping you succeed in this business.

If you are new to this particular business, then both of these elements will take some time to build. Relationships in particular are certainly not a think that you can build overnight. However, the relationships will come if you are willing to make the investment.

One thing that is more in your immediate control is learning how to sell effectively against your competition. As I mentioned in the sales section, there are so many good books on the sales subject that will help you refine your sales techniques. Over the years I have constantly tried to learn more about sales and become a better sales representative. It is a cycle that never really ends as you can never reach perfection especially since you can count on your competition to always change.

Another part of my everyday life is getting to know my competition and how they operate. When it comes to beating your competition, you want and need to know how they are selling against you so that you can counter. This takes time to uncover but your best resource for uncovering this is from your peers, marketing, and looking at the competitive web-sites to see what components of their product they are highlighting. I want to know what they are telling my customers, where they are pricing, and how they think they are going to win the business.

Strangely enough, there is another form of competition that I face daily and that comes internally within my company. Most companies typically create an environment that fosters "healthy" internal competition. Consequently, it is structured in such a way that you are competing against others in the company for better sales numbers and for that coveted number one position on the sales charts.

Some companies have a cut throat culture where you feel an aggressiveness and almost hostility from fellow representatives but most companies have a culture where everyone is on the same team and people support each other.

Even so, you don't want to find yourself at the bottom of a sales performance roster so there is always motivation to keep your business as healthy as possible and better than that territory next to you.

THE OFFICE

There are many people that have the assumption that all of the medical device and pharmaceutical companies have local corporate offices that the staff reports to. In reality, most companies have only a couple of regional offices that you see very rarely unless you happen to live close to one.

Thus, your office is typically your home office. Or many times, your vehicle where you will spend much of your time.

Having a home office is nice for those days when you don't have to see customers since it means that you can get straight to work without any commute. However, if you have never worked out of a home office before, it does take discipline.

First, you have to have the discipline to get into your office at the same time you would if you had to report to a traditional office. While you could hit that snooze button another time, there is always much to be done and so getting up and going at the same time or earlier is important.

Then, you need to tune out all possible distractions so that you can be as productive as possible throughout the day. Whether it is the TV, game consoles, housework, etc., these are all distractions that must wait until you are finished with your day.

However, if you are anything like me, you may find that you are far more productive in your home office than in a traditional office since I find the formal work offices to have too many distractions. It seems that there are so many side conversations within the office and more meetings since people see each other more. My home office is a place where it is quiet and I can focus.

However, for some new parents, you may find that you are more productive working at the local coffee shop or hospital lobby.

People often ask me, how often do I work in my office? Well every morning before I leave for customer sites, I pull up my laptop, answer emails, do a quote, and prepare for the day. I also do a little more work when I arrive back to my office from the day. However, I usually reserve one full day a week to working in my office to catch up on all of the things going on during the week that take time.

Things vary though, some people work two or three days in their office. I recall when I was in pharmaceuticals sales, I spent a little more time in my office per day as most of my schedule revolved around mid day activities such as "Lunch and Learn" meetings. It really depends on your territory and product, and so the amount of time you spend will vary for you. It is about finding the right balance and maximizing your effectiveness.

TYPICAL DAY

Many people have asked me to describe a typical day. This is a bit difficult to do since a typical day is not so typical. However, this is an important question so let me do my best to describe it.

First, your typical day starts the day before with some planning. Since you want to optimize your day out, you need to make a plan as to where you need to go the next day. So hypothetically lets say you need to talk with three doctors in the morning, you have a lunch appointment at noon, and then you want to do some cold calling in the afternoon as well as check on an installation that is taking place.

Planning Tip: when I do my planning, I always use software to help. I map it out first in a program called MapPoint (from Microsoft) to create a route and then I put it on my Outlook calendar. This will allow me to maximize my time in the field and not waste any time trying to figure out where to go next. It also allows me to optimize my route so I am as efficient as possible.

I get up early and go into my home office with some coffee to knock out some email messages and ensure

I have all necessary literature for the day, take time to review previous contact notes for all appointments for the day. Depending on where I am going, I time my departure so I can be at my first appointment at about 8:00 AM.

If my first appointment is a doctor, I go to their office, check-in with the front desk, and usually wait. These doctors are usually seeing you in-between patients so I have learned to be patient but make use of the time by using my smart phone to answer or send work related emails.

Once I get to see the physician, I know my time is limited so I push my agenda but spin my information so the physician understands why they should be listening. You are also looking for any other opportunities to expand your business with them. After the appointment is over, I take some notes, and head to my second, third, etc.

In pharmaceuticals, you will pay particular attention to the staff of the office and will work to build relationships with them as well. As anyone in pharmaceutical sales will tell you, the front desk is your gateway to the rest of the office so be very nice.

Let's say my lunch appointment is a product presentation by a customer that is interested in replacing an older piece of equipment. In my case, my presentations were always accompanied by a specialist. Thus, I show up at the hospital and meet my specialist at the agreed upon time. We would then sign-in, and head to the department.

For this example, let's say this meeting was with Surgery. Thus, we would then report to the office of the surgery director or the conference room where the meeting is going to be held.

The presentation could last anywhere from ten minutes to two hours depending on what we are talking about. I would say that typical medical device presentations are about an hour.

Also, the number of people coming in for the meeting could vary from one to a dozen and can range from tech's, doctors, directors, biomed, purchasing, etc. It all depends on your product and the particular situation.

In many presentations, you will find that the physicians tend to only pop in for a very limited time (usually ten minutes right in the middle of your presentation). Thus, you need to be prepared to give the accelerated version to them while not losing the rest of the audience.

Presentations usually consist of a product overview, configuration discussions, why this product is superior to anything else on the market, pricing, and Q&A.

Once the presentation is finished and wrapped up, I normally would visit my other contacts within the hospital before leaving. I just want to maintain contact with these other people and determine if there were any other opportunities that I could participate in.

Once I have done everything I set out to do in the hospital, I sign out, and head back to my vehicle to take notes, answer voicemails, check email, etc. Then it is on to my next stop on my list.

While I am driving, I am calling other people in the company (such as service) to solve problems or check on repair status, as well as other customers to answer questions or check-in.

If I have an installation going on or a recent installation, I will stop in and see how things are progressing. Are there any problems, needs, or action items that need to be addressed? Is there anything that may compromise the success of the project or my customers satisfaction? Assuming things are well, I can continue upon my day.

Once I am finished with my appointments and cold calling, I return to the office for more documentation into the CRM (Customer Resource Management tool) and beginning the planning for the next day.

Some days may be very different from this one but I would say that this is a pretty typical day. The schedule is not that different from pharmaceutical to medical device sales with the exception of the installations.

The gist of it is pretty simple, you are merely touching base with customers to determine needs, build relationships, and see where you can further develop the business.

COVERING A HOSPITAL

If you have never covered a hospital before, it can be intimidating at first. There are so many different departments, so much chaos, and you don't know where anything is when you first walk in. So let's simplify it for a moment.

Before you cover a hospital, you need to go through a credentialing process. In the late 1990's, hospitals started widely using third party companies to help them clear the people that are walking into these facilities. These credentialing companies charge the vendors an annual fee, you will have to fill out some information, and then they will issue you a user ID and password used to sign in when at the facilities. Hospitals like this service because it keep records of your entry, ensures that all of your inoculations are up to date, ensures that you have identification when in a facility, etc. It is just a more controlled process.

Any sales representative will tell you that the process is cumbersome but we all must do it. It is a necessary evil of the business and there really is no way around it.

Once you have signed up with the credentialing system that a hospital uses (if you are unclear, hospital purchasing will tell you which one they use), you then need to sign in every time you visit a hospital.

Where you sign in depends on the location. When you enter a hospital through the main lobby, there is typically a small kiosk that you will access to sign in. This may be in the lobby, or sometimes it is located in purchasing (AKA, Materials Management) but it is usually in one of those two places. Once you are signed in, the kiosk usually prints a badge that you wear as you head to your destination within the hospital.

When you are in a hospital, there are so many people that you would like to see. From Purchasing, Executives, Department Managers, Doctors, Technicians, Biomed, etc. You can literally spend an entire day working one hospital. However, what shortens this timeline is that most of these people won't have time to talk with you without an appointment and most of these people won't give you an appointment unless you have something that is important to discuss with them (that interests them).

Thus, you do what you can. Stop by, learn what you can from whoever you can, and begin making a name for yourself. The first few times will be frustrating as you know no one and vice versa. However, as you show up more and more, you will get to know these people and will even become friends with many of them. I can recall being somewhat of a fixture in some of my institutions after a couple of years of relationship building and some large transactions.

Also, some departments are highly protected and so you can't just walk into them. For instance, you would never walk into a operating area since you have to have proper clearance and proper attire (scrubs, shoe covers, etc.). You would also not waltz into an ICU, cath lab, NICU, maternity ward, or the like. You have to be careful not to violate the hospitals guidelines or compromise patience privacy or you will find yourself banned from the facility.

When having a difficult time gaining access, representatives will often call and/or email the facility instead. It is often times much easier to get an email response than to try to get unannounced calendar time with a customer.

Another gateway for access is through your service organization. You can always accompany one of your service engineers when they are on-site to repair a piece of equipment that belongs to your company. It gives you a reason for being there.

As you build relationships and installed base with a hospital, your access will vastly improve. However, in the beginning you have to be patient and do the best that you can.

TRACKING SALES AND NOTES (CRM)

Almost all companies use some sort of CRM (Customer Resource Management System). Whether it is Salesforce, Siebel, etc., there is a system where you will be expected to take daily notes about your interactions with your customers. This is an important task because it allows you to keep on track with what you are doing so you don't get accounts and conversations mixed up. Believe me when I tell you that it is very easy to get conversations and details interchanged when you are busy. Consequently, this (typically) mandatory daily activity is very useful for you too.

Another important part of note taking is for transparency. Your managers are not with you on a daily basis but need to know what you are doing, who you are talking with, and what you are discussing. If you are not taking notes, it is very difficult for them to keep up with you and the other representatives that they oversee.

Some people choose to keep more detailed notes outside of the CRM as well. In my mind, the more information that you can document, the easier it is to stay organized (which is of the utmost importance in this job).

I usually spend about five minutes per visit taking notes so it is not a very large commitment. I also try to do so immediately after leaving a site so all of the important details are fresh in my mind.

Learning how to navigate your company's CRM systems is sometimes the toughest part of this activity since some of them are not clearly and efficiently executed. However, most CRM systems have an on-line tutorial that will help you become more proficient with the system and its functions.

PRODUCT SPECIALISTS

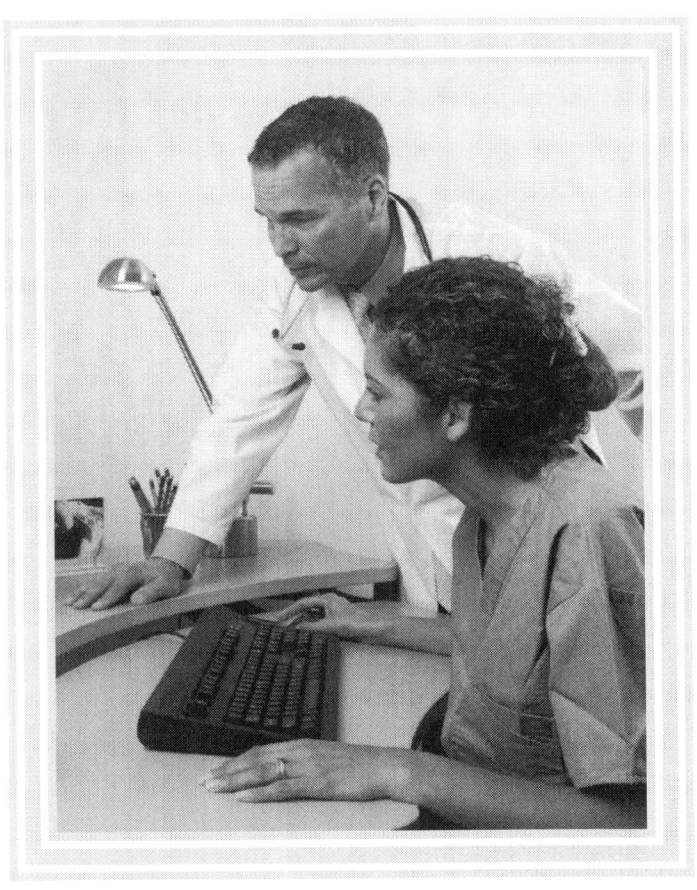

Depending on what you sell and the complexity of the product, you very well may have a Product Sales Specialist. Many Sales Representatives are considered Account Managers or "Quarterbacks" that are responsible for managing the customers, building relationships, ensuring customer satisfaction, driving revenue, etc. However, many times, you are not expected to be the foremost expert for the product.

When you are working with a customer on a complex product sale, presentations will frequently be done by the sales specialist. A product specialist is tasked with knowing the product and clinical material intricately so that they can help you be successful in a sale. These are people that typically have a clinical background so they can easily talk the talk of the clinical users. Also, since many of the specialists have worked in the area that they specialize at one point in their career, they are acutely aware of the common challenges or obstacles that the customers may experience in workflow, equipment, etc.

Sales Specialists are very important people to have on your team and when you win, they win (and vice versa). They also are ultimately accountable for growing the business in their geography which usually spans over several sales representatives.

At many of the Pharmaceutical companies and many smaller medical device companies, you are the sales specialist in addition to being sales person. You are responsible for knowing the product, the competition, and how your product can be of use to the customer. Pharmaceutical companies are particularly well known for offering very advanced training that prepares you for this role. This is very important for the Pharmaceutical representatives since the face time with any given physician is extremely limited. Thus, when a question is posed by a physician, I needed to know the answer on the spot.

MEETINGS

Meetings are a part of any company and a part of everyone's regular schedule. Besides your customer meetings, you will typically be responsible for attending weekly, regional, and national meetings.

Weekly meetings are generally conference calls that discuss business updates, review opportunities, discuss strategies, etc. They can also contain short training sessions and much more. These are typically only an hour or so long and usually occur in the beginning on the week (Monday morning is a favorite). They are pretty informal but they allow the Regional Manager to touch base with his team as an entire unit on a weekly basis.

Regional meetings are typically held a couple of times a year in a central location and will usually span a day or two. Depending on the company, your region could consist of half of the United States, or just a couple of hundred miles. These meetings are more general in nature but they typically discuss regional performance, business updates, product updates, and are frequently accompanied by training. Those attending these meetings will typically include zone managers, your regional sales peers, and some senior leadership.

The National Sales Meetings are the large meetings typically held once a year in a central location or near the company headquarters and extend several days to a week. These meetings are an all hands on deck sort of meeting attended by sales representatives across the country (and many times world). If your company has more than one division, you will generally see all divisions present.

These meetings are attended by the Senior leaders of the company, all sales management, marketing representatives, all sales representatives, specialists, etc. They are very often large productions that can be a lot of fun, motivational, and educational.

Depending on your company size, these meetings can be attended by thousands of people and are held at large conference centers. Orlando for instance is very popular. Smaller companies might host them at headquarters.

National sales meetings give the lay of the land, overall company performance, future direction, and much more. You will have a chance to network with other representatives and become acquainted with the company's latest technology.

TRADE SHOWS

Trade Shows are large clinical shows typically held at a convention center in a central place. These shows generally have a clinical theme (Cardiology, Radiology, etc.) and are attended by people from across the healthcare industry to learn about new treatments, technology, and more.

Most major pharmaceutical companies and medical device companies attend at least one of these shows every year and construct elaborate booths.

At some point in your career, you will probably be asked to help represent the company at one of these shows by standing in the booth to field questions by customers, hand out information, and take down leads (i.e. the name, number, and organization of interested customers).

The trade shows usually span several days and will unquestionably leave your feet aching at the end. However, they are a good place to learn more about products, network with others, and have a change of pace from your ordinary responsibilities.

SALES FUNNEL

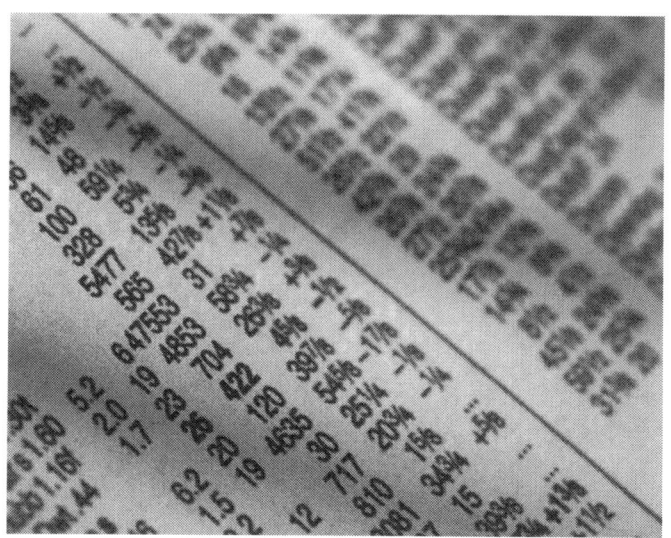

Most every company will have what is considered a sales funnel. A sales funnel is what is used to help you, and your managers keep track of business opportunities over the next several years. What is tracked for each opportunity varies but typically it will include the following:

- Customer Name
- Product name
- Quote Number
- Quantity
- Expected Close Date
- Expected Revenue
- Competition
- Likelihood of Winning
- Customer Contact Information
- Notes Pertaining to the Sale
- Won, Loss, or In Progress

- Reason for Win/Loss

There is a lot more that can be tracked but this is generally what is included for each sales opportunity for most companies.

Within the sales funnel, there are usually tools that allow managers to aggregate data, run reports, and help create forecasts.

Since sales are the lifeblood to any company, these funnels are taken very seriously by everyone that touches it. Part of your job is to make regular updates to the data to ensure that management has the best possible picture of your business and the business of others in the company. Typically we are making updates, additions, or changes to the funnel on a daily basis.

Your manager and possibly specialists will regularly review your funnel with you. Regularly may mean once a week or possibly once a month depending on the organization.

Generally, these reviews are looking at how your funnel is trending (is it growing or shrinking), do you have enough business to achieve your quota, and where are there gaps.

Funnel maintenance is just another part of your daily routine. It doesn't take long and is an important task that must be done.

QUOTES

For medical device sales, when a customer wants pricing on a piece of equipment, it is drawn up on an official company quote.

Quoting equipment can be simple or extremely complex depending on exactly what you are dealing with. Some pieces of equipment have hundreds of different options and configurations while others have only a few. Ensuring that your quotes correct is very dependent on understanding the needs of your customers.

The net pricing of your equipment is frequently determined on pre-negotiated contracts with National Buying Groups often referred to as a GPO. Hospitals and physician practices sign up with the buying groups to take advantage of the terms and conditions of the buying group as well as their pricing. In return, the buying groups are paid a percentage by the manufacturers of the equipment being sourced.

So for instance, the list price of your widget is $100 but the buying group discount for this hospital entitles them to a 15% discount. Thus the net price is $85.00.

If your company's payment terms are Net 10 but the buying group is Net 30, then the customer received the Net 30 terms.

These groups make it much easier for everyone involved as the price is generally set for a product and it speeds negotiations.

So one of the first things (other than configuration) that you will need to understand when quoting is what buying group or groups the institution is affiliated with.

Depending on your company, you may be required to fill out your own quotes, or you may have a department that aids in the process. In some companies, quotes can even be built into the CRM.

Regardless of how it is generated, once the quote is completed, it is your job to ensure that it is accurate before presenting it to your customer.

For hospitals, quotes are frequently requested well before a sale (as much as a year in advance) so that a customers can budget for the piece of equipment. Each department gathers quotes for equipment they need and then creates a wish list. It is up to administration to determine what does or does not make it into the final budget for purchases within that fiscal year.

It is not until it has been approved that your customer will be able to move forward on an acquisition.

SALES

There are many good books on the subject of sales and sales techniques (*Miller Heiman* and Neil Rackham's *Spin Selling* are both good books on the subject) so I will not recreate the wheel in this book. However, the sales process is partially about technology, partially about price, and partially about the sales representative.

You may have the best product in the world but perhaps you don't have the relationships with the physicians to help you move it. Or perhaps you have a great product but you heavily over configured it leaving you priced much higher than your competition. Or maybe you have a good price and a good product but the customer just doesn't know you very well and isn't comfortable buying from you. These scenarios are always in flux so it is your job to optimize your position regardless of the situation.

One of the most important things to remember in sales is that people buy from people. You don't have to be the best looking or funniest person in the world but you want to be genuine, professional, and likable.

When you have someone interested in your product, it may be as simple as providing a quote to get a sale, however, most times it will take much more including an in depth presentation to educate the customer on why your solution is the best.

In a hospital, once a decision for an approved piece of capital equipment has been made, it must be signed off on by department managers and administration. Only after all signatures are required is it ready to make its way to the purchasing department. However, be prepared as the purchasing department that will issue the order to your company will probably want some last minute concessions.

In an office, a decision for a medical device product could be made the same day with little to no hassle. You provide a quote and a purchase agreement is issued.

For pharmaceuticals, the decision a physician makes to write and recommend your product can be immediate but the aggregate results will only be realized over time.

So it really depends on what you are representing. It is certainly more complicated in a hospital since you have so many different buying influences, however, despite the complexity, hospitals are worth the investment of time since they are a good source of constant revenue.

One thing is for sure, you deal with a lot of different personality types in this business. Physicians have a reputation for being difficult to work with and this absolutely something that you will contend with on a regular basis. Some people will be very nice, some will be neutral, and some will give you a hard time. Dealing with these personalities is part of the job and your ability to sort them all out and maintain a good relationship is why you get to earn as much as you do.

A good thing to remember, it is just business so don't take it personally. Keep your eyes on the fiscal prize and it will make dealing with any of these personalities much easier.

IMAGE AND PROFESSIONALISM

Image and professionalism are a given in the business. If you are reading this book, you are probably also reading Daniel Riley's *How to Get a Medical Device Sales Job* so there is no need to reinvent the wheel.

Suffice it to say, image is very important to these companies and you are the outward affiliation to the company. So in a day in the life of me, I take the time to exercise, dress and groom properly.

Every day you are in front of a customer, you are building an image and you want this image to be as favorable as possible.

VACATION

This job is a lot of fun but like any job, you will need a vacation. The good news is that the medical device and pharmaceutical companies are usually pretty liberal in their vacation allotments. You accrue vacation as you work and usually have about two weeks per year during the first few years.

After you are employed for a while and gain tenure, your vacation allowance increases. Some companies give eight to ten weeks of vacation for their most seasoned representatives. It is a nice perk but there is a catch.

The big catch is that you are still responsible for your quota even while you are on vacation. While you can typically find someone to field your calls while you are gone, your quota does not go on hold just because you are at the beach.

This means that many sales people are frequently still in touch with their business and customers while they are gone. However, if you are a good planner, you probably scheduled everything to account for your vacation and cleared your To Do list as much as possible.

It is very important to shut down the engines and take your vacation or you will experience burn out. Thus, you will find that most sales representatives do a good job of using their vacation time to recharge their batteries and come back stronger.

EXPENSES

You can't talk about a day in the life without talking about expenses as this is a business with costs.

Upon employment, you are issued a corporate card for all company related expenses as well as a thick copy of the expense policy. While the policies vary, all expenses do have to have a business purpose.

There are also government regulations (such as the Sunshine Act) that prohibit excessive wining and dining of physicians and customers.

Typical expenses will be parking, phone bills, certain meals or entertainment, tolls, office supplies, vendor credentialing fee's, etc. If you are traveling overnight, your meals, hotel, airfare, etc. will also be valid expenses.

The rule of thumb with any company is to use good judgment and keep your expenses reasonable.

Tracking your expenses will be done by gathering receipts for your purchases and submitting them through an expense tracking system on a weekly or bi-weekly basis. Typically you will need to itemize your expenses, include purpose, scan copies of your receipts, and submit them into the electronic system for management approval. Once they are approved, you are reimbursed via a direct deposit.

If you are working for a very small company, expense guidelines will most likely be tighter and you may not have the electronic tracking mechanisms.

No matter how you look at it, expenses are carefully watched by these companies so you always want to ensure that you are in compliance.

SUMMARY

The day of a pharmaceutical rep or medical device sales person is unquestionably fast paced and ever changing. It is a fun and glamorous industry that is one of the most highly sought after jobs in business.

One of the things that makes a strong representative is a great attitude. You stand to make a lot of money in this business, so there will naturally be some associated stress which is inherent with any sales job. It is up to you to manage this stress and keep your focus on what matters; Getting your job done, keeping the customers happy, and making lots of money.

Every day is a bit different and every company is different. However, this grand tour of the business should give you a good overall sense of what it is like to be in this business and some of the things that you will encounter in this field.

I wish you the best in your career and hope you enjoy it!

Made in the USA
Lexington, KY
03 June 2013